IMAGES OF SCOTLAND

UDDINGSTON

IMAGES OF SCOTLAND

UDDINGSTON

HELEN MOIR

TEMPUS

Frontispiece: Peter and Susan Murphy at their wedding reception at
Devonshire Gardens Hotel, Glasgow. The couple were married on
the 27 September 1998 in America and reside at Easter Farm in
Uddingston. They have been very supportive during my preparation
of this book and are great friends of both my husband Bill and I.
This book is dedicated to them and their family.

First published 2007

Tempus Publishing Limited
The Mill, Brimscombe Port,
Stroud, Gloucestershire, GL5 2QG
www.tempus-publishing.com

© Helen Moir, 2007

British Library Cataloguing in Publication Data.
A catalogue record for this book is available from the British Library.

ISBN 978 0 7524 4339 3

Typesetting and origination by Tempus Publishing Limited.
Printed in Great Britain.

Contents

Introduction

The town of Uddingston lies a few short miles from the great metropolis of Glasgow, in fact just about thirteen miles from the city centre. The town lies in the ancient and historic Bothwell Parish in the county of what was once industrial Lanarkshire, one of the counties that form the Strathclyde region. The town is situated near the river Clyde, which meanders its way to Glasgow and the Firth of Clyde from its source in the Lead Hills. The famous Clyde which once saw the building of so many great ships; there is a local saying that if one is healthy you are 'Clyde built'.

The name Uddingston comes from the Angles' word 'ton' meaning homestead combined with the name Ud, or Od, both words that seem to have been common in the language of these people, who arrived from North Germany and, with the passing of time, joined the tribes of the Celts, Picts, and Britons to form our beloved Scottish nation.

Early history tells us of Walter, who was the son of Rodger Odistoun. Connected also to this gentleman are the names Eddistone, and Ediston. Walter gave his allegiance to Edward I of England, a ruthless king also known as Edward Longshanks or 'Hammer of the Scots'. Edward at this time was in control of much of Scotland. Years later, in 1314, his son Edward was defeated by Robert the Bruce at Bannockburn.

We know there was a Bronze Age settlement at Uddingston. Pieces of urns from the period were found in 1885 when houses were being erected at Kyle Park. This would have been seen as a convenient place for the ease of crossing the Clyde with prime farming land and good fishing in the river. The Romans were in Uddingston and played a part in the area's history. Relations between them and the local tribes seem to have been harmonious and there were intermarriages. The Antoine Wall, built by the Romans to keep the unconquerable Picts at bay, stretched from the Forth to the Clyde estuaries, from one side of Scotland to the other, below and often referred to as The Cradle of Christianity. It was a part of Scotland from where messages carried by early saints and missionaries spread through what was otherwise dark tribal Scotland. The Roman road from England ran through Uddingston, journeying through Motherwell and reaching Tannochside through Bothwellhaugh (The Pallis) and Fallside, reaching the Antoine Wall at Dumbarton. Until much later, when the construction of General Wade's turnpike roads opened up previously inaccessible areas, the Roman road remained the only properly constructed road.

The Parish of Bothwell had ruling families. David I of Scotland, 1124–1153, built many churches in Scotland, completing the work begun by his mother Queen Margaret in the Romanisation of the church. For his loyalty and service to the king the lands of Bothwell were granted to David de Olifard or Oliphant. He erected a castle at Bothwell although it was probably not on the site of the later castle built in the thirteenth century by Walter Murray, who by this time had inherited the lands. The great Scottish patriot William Wallace, according to legend and along with Robert the Bruce whose sister was married into the Murray family, probably stayed or passed through the district. Edward I conquered the castle after a siege with an army of nearly seven thousand men in 1301. After the Battle of Bannockburn in 1314 the castle was surrendered to Edward Bruce, brother of the king, who ordered it to be dismantled.

In the year 1361 Joan Murray married into the powerful Douglas family. Archibald Douglas, 'The Grim' or 'Black Douglas' played a large part in the success of his king Robert the Bruce. Womenfolk in England apparently sang a lullaby to their children about him: 'Hush ye, hush ye, the Black Douglas shall not get thee'! In 1362 Douglas restored the castle but on a much less grand scale. It was eventually abandoned in the seventeenth century and a new mansion built close by using stones from the castle. Later in the nineteenth century it came into the ownership of the Earl of Home, family of Sir Alec Douglas Home, British Prime Minister, who renounced his earldom. In 1926 the new castle was demolished like so many other grand buildings in the area.

Commercial activity in the earlier years was predominantly farming by the Douglas family and with their tenants such as Rae, Cross, Scott, Jack and Wilkie. At the turn of the nineteenth century John Wilkie began the manufacturing of ploughs in Uddingston. Scotland was changing rapidly with a better road system and with the advent of the Industrial Revolution canals were built carrying produce to markets at home and abroad much faster. New rotational farming systems improved production. New improvement in farm implements, such as Wilkie's plough, helped to ease the back-breaking work done by man and beast.

In 1846 the population of Uddingston was 703 and a main source of employment was cottage handloom weaving which employed whole families in their homes. The advent of mill and factory caused the demise of this craft.

In time, like other Lanarkshire villages, coalmining became a major source of employment. Until nationalisation the pit's owners offered mostly poor pay and horrendous working conditions. In and around Uddingston with the advance of heavy industry such as pig iron, coal and steel production, Lanarkshire became the industrial belt of Scotland. In neighbouring Coatbridge and Motherwell, permanent palls of smoke hung around the towns. Pits around Uddingston included Haughhead, Bothwell Castle, Bothwell Park, Viewpark, Bredisholm, Tannochside, and Newton. The latter was the last one in the area to close, in 1964. Little or nothing can now be seen on the horizon to show this once bustling industry. I still feel very proud of my own mining family background and of the people who lived and shared the joys and sorrows together with great tenacity and humour. Folk came to this area from Ireland, Lithuania and Poland in search of work and married and settled, usually quite amicably, into existing communities.

By 1849 the railway to Uddingston was completed and still forms an important link today. Trams arrived in Uddingston in 1907 from the Caledonian station to the cross. The Lanarkshire Tramway Co.'s trams were nicknamed the 'shooglies'. The trams were gone by 1948. Later the company became the well-known SMT. A noted business family in Uddingston, here for many generations, and still going strong, is Tunnock's. Their excellent bakery produce goes all over the world – you haven't lived until you've tasted a Tunnock's teacake! Thomas Tunnock, founder of the firm, was born in Uddingston in 1865. As a young man he was apprenticed at the Aberdour Bakery in Old Mill Road and later bought his own premises on Bellshill Road and thus the legend began. Thomas was a community spirited man and did much for local causes, work that was carried on by Archie his son and later by his grandsons. Through the years many from Uddingston and surrounding areas have worked in the bakery.

Another famous business of a later era, sadly now gone, was the American-owned Caterpillar factory, at Tannochside. They were forward thinking with an excellent safety record and in-house medical department, running 'good health' programmes for their workers.

A well-known landmark lies within the Bothwell Parish, situated at Bothwell Bridge, on the river Clyde where it meets with the Calder and the Avon. This monument commemorates the Battle of Bothwell Bridge, fought in 1679, or Clyde Bridge as it was then known. Many fleeing Covenanters were given refuge and safety at Hamilton Palace by Duchess Anne Hamilton. The Covenanters were beaten by the overpowering force of King Charles II led by his illegitimate son, the Duke of Monmouth, and Graham of Claverhouse.

Mary Queen of Scots has associations with the area too through her involvement with the Hamilton family. Mary married James Hepburn, Earl of Bothwell, her third husband and alleged murderer of her second husband, Lord Darnley. No evidence can be found that Mary ever resided at Bothwell Castle, but she did stay at neighbouring Hamilton castles such as Cadzow and Craignethan (Tillietudilum) and Auld Machan. In all possibility Mary could have been at the castle although her husband's own castle was not at Bothwell.

Easter Farm once belonged to the Jack family, and is reputed to be one of the oldest buildings in Uddingston. Originally known as Birkenshaw House, it is now owned by Peter and Susan Murphy. The name Easter Farm was given by a member of the Ford family. The original Easter Farm was on Old Mill Road. The house was built in 1782 by Andrew Jack but prior to this another form of dwelling existed here reputed to be one of the stopping places used in 1746 by Bonnie Prince Charlie on the disastrous retreat from Derby that finished on the field of Culloden. The owners of the dwelling hid the horses by covering them in sharking and removing them to a lower field in case they should be commandeered.

The Jack family have, like many other names in Uddingston, a lineage in the area going back many centuries. These families were often farmers beholden to the Bothwell estate. In old records they are noted as 'vassals'. Other local names are Caidwell, Scott, Wilkinson, Pettigrew, Braidwood, Silverton, Wilson, and Crosby.

Acknowledgements

I would like to thank the following people and institutions for photographs and information: Margaret and John Lyth, Mr Boyd Tunnock, Ann and Tom Sneden, Janet Knox, Norman Robson, Norah and Ronnie Porteous, Motherwell Heritage Centre (Brian Kirk, Margaret McGarry, Steven Preston), *Hamilton Advertiser*, *Motherwell Times* (Robert Wilson), *Bellshill Speaker* (Michael McQuaid), Uddingston Cricket Club (James Lockhart), Iain Margaret Fergusson and John Guthrie.

A very special thank you to Margaret Lyth, whose extensive superb collection of postcards graciously donated for this book along with her expert knowledge has played a marvellous part in the completion of this book.

I thank Peter and Susan Murphy and Cllr Andrew Burns and his wife Margaret for their wonderful support during the preparation of this book. Lastly, I give a special thank you to my husband Bill for his unfailing love and support.

one

The Castle

Bothwell Castle. The name Bothwell is derived from Middle English *bothe wiel* or *wael*, Old English *woel*, a booth or 'hut by the eddy' or fish pool. The castle was built in the thirteenth century by Walter de Moravia, known as Walter Murray. The Murray family were great supporters of both William Wallace and Robert the Bruce. Edward I, ('Edward Longshanks'), the 'Hammer of the Scots' laid siege to it in 1301, with an army of nearly 7,000 men. Robert the Bruce ordered its dismantling after the Battle of Bannockburn in 1314, and in 1362 it was restored by the 'Black Douglas', Archibald. The castle was abandoned in the seventeenth century when the new one was built close by using stones from it. (courtesy Margaret Lyth)

Bothwell Castle from the west bank of the River Clyde. After its dismantling in 1314 it was recaptured by the English under Edward III in 1336 and rebuilt only to be taken again by the Scots in 1337 when it was dismantled for a second time. In 1594 it is recorded that 'erection of the idolatry of the Mass had taken place at Bothwell Castle, and the owners, the Maxwells, were thus regarded as traitors. Sir Walter Scott wrote these lovely words when visiting the new castle, 'Full where the copse wood opens wild, Thy pilgrim step hath staid, Where Bothwell's towers in ruins piles o'erlook the verdant glade.'

This old postcard view shows Bothwell Castles, old and new, at Uddingston, and shows how close they were to each other. The Barony of Bothwell was acquired in marriage by Archibald the Grim, third Earl of Douglas. The Black Douglas's forfeited the castle in 1455, when it reverted back to the Crown. In 1492 it passed into the ownership of the Red Douglas's in whose possession it remained until the late nineteenth century when it passed by marriage to the Home family. The new castle was demolished in 1926 when in the ownership of the Douglas-Home family. (courtesy Ann and Tom Sneden)

Bothwell Castle, Uddingston.

This old postcard view shows new Bothwell Castle in around 1904. The castle was built around the end of the seventeenth century. The two wings were built first from stone from the old castle, and only some years later was the central part completed with stone from a local quarry. (courtesy Margaret Lyth)

This old postcard view shows the interior of Bothwell Castle. Built by Walter Olifard or Oliphant, Sheriff of Lothian, during the reign of Alexander II, it changed hands several times prior to 1455 when it passed to Andrew Murray of Bothwell who married Christian, sister to Robert the Bruce, victor of Bannockburn in 1314. It is reputed that Archibald the Grim offered to fight no fewer than five English knights in single combat who aspired to the hand in marriage of Joanna, the sole heiress of the Morays' Murray. Joanna was the granddaughter of Moray of Bothwell, Warden of Scotland during the minority reign of David II, and Christian, the sister of Robert the Bruce. Margaret Lyth (who kindly loaned this postcard) remembers Mr Innes, the custodian, chastising children, including her, for climbing on the old walls!

An aerial view of Bothwell Castle, c. 1990. The castle was once owned by the Earl of Bothwell, third husband of the ill-fated Mary Queen of Scots. James Hepburn the 4th Earl of Bothwell, was implicated in the murder of Lord Darnley, her second husband, in 1567. The Earl of Bothwell was brought to trial on the 12 of April 1567 but was acquitted. Lord Darnley was the father of the future King James VI of Scotland and first of England, known as, 'The wisest fool in Christendom'. (courtesy of Margaret Lyth)

two

A Walk Around Uddingston

Above: Uddingston Cross and Main Street, *c.* 1936. Uddingston was the last line to go on the Lanarkshire Tramway system. It operated between Motherwell and Uddingston and closed on the 14 February 1931. Apparently the grocer's shop at the Cross always had a cat sitting on the counter. (courtesy Margaret Lyth)

Opposite below: Croftbank Crescent in the early 1900s. The children seem well wrapped up so it must have been a cold day. (courtesy Margaret Lyth)

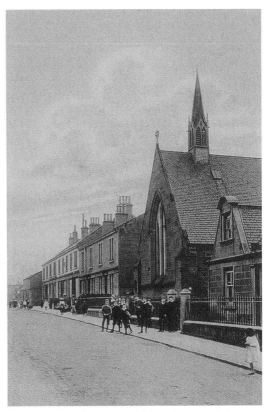

Right: The Congregational church in Old Mill Road, Uddingston, *c.* 1907. It was opened in 1880 and is now used as the village hall. (courtesy Margaret Lyth)

Below: Athol Gardens, Sheepburn Road, *c.* 1904. The message on the reverse of this postcard view says, 'Am here enjoying myself, Annie's house is the one on the left. Dolly and Arthur are on the road.' This card was published by the Edinburgh firm of William Ritchie and Sons, who took photographs of the village some three or four years prior to their appearance as postcards for a book, *Views of Uddingston,* published by Mrs McLeod, the local newsagent. (courtesy Margaret Lyth)

Posted in Uddingston on the 14 May 1908, this postcard view of Clydeford Drive in around 1902 shows haymaking and a nursery in the foreground with cold frames. It shows the rural nature of village life at this time. The Drive now has houses on each side and more houses now occupy the fields and site of the nursery. (courtesy Margaret Lyth)

This postcard view shows Kyle Park Drive. The railings, as in many towns and villages, were removed during the Second World War. Note the poor condition of the road. Margaret Lyth recalls having to go to the house with the flagpole to meet her mother after school in the 1950s when her mother was attending meetings of the Episcopal Church's ladies working party. The group met in turn at houses as there was no church hall. Margaret was deemed to be too young to be given a latchkey to let herself in to the Rectory. The hostess always kept a special 'goody' for her, devoured with relish, as post-war food rationing was still on. (courtesy Margaret Lyth)

Uddingston Station in around 1910. Coal was the most important cargo and passengers were a bonus. The waiting room (right) has now been demolished. The hoarding behind the gas lamp on the right is advertising 'Germoline', an antiseptic ointment. The railways brought much-needed inward investment to the area, allowing better movement of merchandise: as a result the population grew because people could work further away from home and return easily each evening. (courtesy Margaret Lyth)

This view shows Kylepark Crescent from Kylepark Avenue, Uddingston, *c.* 1906. Kyle was the maiden name of the wife of Mr Thomson who built the houses. A Bronze Age urn (*c.* 1500 BC) was found during the construction of the Kylepark houses in 1885. It is now in the Royal Scottish Museum in Edinburgh.

Left: This is Clydeneuk House, Clydeneuk, built in 1857. It was known locally as 'Candyman's Castle' as its owner John Poynter started life as a rag and bone man, exchanging rags and bones for sweets. Margaret Lyth remembers as a child it being used as an old folks' home. She also recalls coming to sing here with her church choir. The house was demolished in 1963. (courtesy Margaret Lyth)

Below: This view made prior to 1905 shows an open aspect looking towards the mock-baronial Clydeneuk House. Sadly now this river bank has become overgrown and has suffered from erosion. (courtesy Margaret Lyth)

Clydeneuk, Uddingston.

The Grammar School was opened next to the Caledonian railway station in 1885. Dominie Smith was appointed the first rector and worked there until his retirement in 1890. Dominie in Old English means teacher. Dominie Smith was a remarkable teacher with a more liberal approach to discipline. He came to Uddingston in 1844, taking a great interest in village life. He was secretary of the Educational Institute of Scotland and an honorary L.L.D Degree was conferred upon him by Glasgow University for his sterling service to education. Extensions were built in 1961-62 and again in 1994, affecting the appearance of Gardenside Street. The sandstone arch dated 1906 was demolished. James S. Walker was rector in the 1950s and early '60s. (courtesy Margaret Lyth)

This is Gardenside Avenue, looking north, *c.* 1906. This postcard was published by William Ritchie and Sons of Edinburgh, a rival of Mr A. Brown of Lanark who published the 'Brown's Series' of postcards. This view has changed little. (courtesy Margaret Lyth)

This old postcard of Powburn Toll in Glasgow Road was posted in Uddingston on September 14 1908. Tolls were abolished in 1878 and the Powburn toll house was strategically situated here on the main road to Carlisle. The toll house became Uddingston's first police station and a second one was built next to St Andrew's rectory in 1924 so for some years Uddingston had the luxury of two police stations. Powburn Toll was demolished in 1973 to make way for the motorway. (courtesy Margaret Lyth)

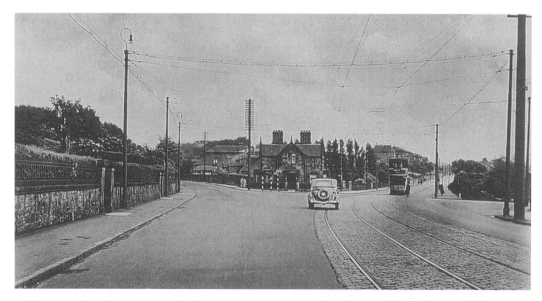

This scene was taken for postcard publishers Valentine and Sons of Dundee and was registered with them in 1936. Alderside House (left of the toll house) was demolished in 1968 to make way for the M74 motorway. There is a Glasgow tram in the distance and a horse and cart can also be seen. The registration number of the car in the foreground is YS8858. (courtesy Margaret Lyth)

This tranquil scene on the river Clyde was published as a postcard by E. Fraser, the niece of Peter Fraser, the stationer, printer and newsagent of Laurelbank, Uddingston. Miss Fraser ran a newsagent in Loanhead Mansions near to Tunnock's present shop in the Main Street. (courtesy Margaret Lyth)

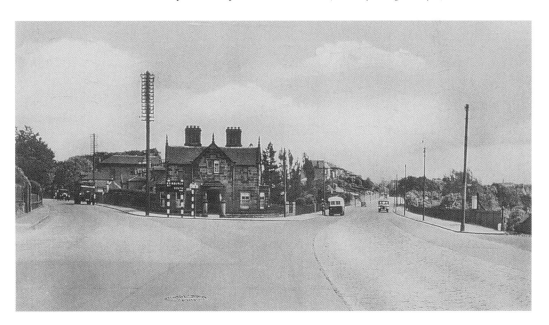

This picture must have been taken after 1948 as the tram's stopped then and the lines lifted. The New Edinburgh Road to the left was a turnpike road built around 1830. Despite the earlier date of the photograph this postcard was sent to Canada on 10 August 1963. (courtesy Margaret Lyth)

The boathouse for the ferry was situated on the Blantyre side of the river Clyde. The adjacent land was also farmed by the ferryman and is still known as 'Boatland'. The cottage in the centre is built in the typical Scottish style known as 'two ee's and a mou' (two eyes and a mouth). This is one of 'Brown's Series' of postcards. (courtesy Margaret Lyth)

This postcard of the boathouse was issued by William Ritchie and Son, Edinburgh, the photograph being taken in around 1902. By the year 2000 the banks of the river had suffered from serious erosion.

The Clyde ferry making the crossing to the Blantyre side of the river. Nothing now remains of the boathouse and cottages. The Clyde begins its journey in Lead Hills further south, meandering its way through both once-industrial and rural Lanarkshire to the great metropolis which is Glasgow.

There was no bridge over the River Clyde in the district except for Bothwell Bridge until the Red (Haughhead) Bridge was built in 1840 to take place of the ford. Ferry Road was a continuation of Gardenside Street. The ferry ceased operation in the early 1920s but prior to that you could hail it by shouting 'Boat'. (courtesy Margaret Lyth)

The house on the right was occupied by the ferryman who was also the farmer. The house was dated 1667 and was there until a few years after the last war. At the time of writing few of the trees that are seen here in front of the cottages remain. Some were blown down in the storm of December 1998. (courtesy Margaret Lyth)

This old postcard, posted in Uddingston on the 25 July 1904, shows the final stages of the replacement Clyde Bridge being built. The girders have now reached the west bank of the river Clyde, the work being done from east to west. A crane can be seen to the left of the picture. (courtesy Margaret Lyth)

Today, only the superstructure of the old bridge remains and to the south a new footbridge has been built. The 1904 is still in use by Scot rail. Note the company of gentlemen standing to the right of the photograph. (courtesy Margaret Lyth)

There was a ferry to the Blantyreferme side of the River Clyde. This path along the riverside was allowed to fall into disrepair by the Clyde Calder's Environmental Project workers under an employment training scheme – what a pity. Many a courtship in times past would have blossomed walking through this beautiful spot. (courtesy Margaret Lyth)

This view of Kyle Park probably dates from the inter-war years. The house with the flagpole in Kyle Park Drive belonged to a Mrs Fitzpatrick during the 1950s. The street entrance to the left of the picture is what is now Clydeford Drive. Kyle Park was laid out in 1882. (courtesy Margaret Lyth)

A view of Kyle Park from the 1900s. The large field, the Langlands, was not finished until after the Second World War and is now occupied by Lawrence houses. As the nineteenth century progressed, Uddingston became ringed by collieries and it was not such a desirable place for Victorian and Edwardian families to come to settle. The building of villas with gardens virtually stopped. Kyle Park was left with an unfinished look and a field in the middle. (courtesy of Margaret Lyth)

Main Street, looking north, *c.* 1905. The buildings on the right have now gone. This view was taken before the arrival of the trams in 1906. Gardenside Street, still sometimes known as 'Latta's Brae' from T. Latta's off-sales grocer's shop on the corner can be seen. This is still a shop but no longer used as a grocery. Opposite can be seen Osbourne Café where truants from Uddingston Grammar went to avoid lessons. Margaret Lyth confesses to being one of them! (courtesy Margaret Lyth)

Posted in Uddingston in 1906 this old postcard shows two ladies posing for the camera at the junction of Edinburgh Road. The North British Railway Bridge can be seen in the background. The railway line ran behind the houses on the left. The name Powburn is derived from Lowland Scots, 'a sluggish stream', and is a softened form of pool. (courtesy Margaret Lyth)

The photograph on this postcard was registered at Valentines of Dundee in 1899. The toll house in front of the villas (right) was at one time the police station. The villas housed some of Uddingston's more affluent citizens and looked out onto fields. In 1966 construction of the M74 motorway began. This was completed two years later and its route cut right through the bottom of this picture changing the view dramatically. (courtesy Margaret Lyth)

Powburn Toll is seen on the right of this card posted 30th December 1903. The gateposts for 'Southend' can be seen. This house is still there but some neighbouring houses were demolished to make way for the construction of the motorway in 1968. (courtesy Margaret Lyth)

This postcard calls the street 'New Road' but it is now known as Crofthead Street. The houses had only recently been built when the picture was taken, prior to 1906. The Victoria Hall (demolished in the early 1930s) was opposite these flats in the distance. (courtesy Margaret Lyth)

This card was wrongly captioned by the publishers. It should read 'Woodlands, Uddingston Road Bothwell'. These houses were built during the inter-war years as part of the 'Home for Heroes' scheme. Note the Lanarkshire Tramways Co. tram in the distance. (courtesy Margaret Lyth)

Spindlehowe Road, *c.* 1910. (courtesy Margaret Lyth)

This view of Bellshill Road in around 1920 is barely recognisable today. The buildings on the left-hand side of the road have been demolished. The picture pre-dates the erection of the Community Centre. The top flat of the house nearest the camera was occupied by the late Mrs Crawford who was a faithful member of St Andrew's Scottish Episcopal church and who baked for the annual sale of work. Her husband worked for Wise's Garage.

Main Street, looking south, *c.* 1902. The corner to the right of this picture used to be known as 'Gow's Corner' because of Gow's grocery shop at the corner of Church Street. Dr Crawford's surgery was opposite. I remember working as a teenager in the 1960s in Cockburn's chemist where Mr Harthill was my boss and Mr Whitcock, from Hamilton, his assistant. (courtesy Margaret Lyth)

Lanarkshire Tramway Co. tram No. 51 is seen here outside Laurelbank. The shop to the far left is now a newsagent. The last Lanarkshire tram to Uddingston ran from Motherwell on the 14 February 1931. The Tramway Co. also ran buses and changed its name to the Lanarkshire Traction Co. The large poster on the tram window advertises various entertainments available in Motherwell which include 'Midnight Madness,' 'Hot Heels' and 'Give and Take'. Also note Player's Navy Cut Cigarettes, without a filter tip.

Uddingston Cross is pictured here in around 1902 from the Bellshill Road. The pillar box was relocated during the late 1990s. This area still has shops but trading in different goods. Uddingston, like many other towns and villages in earlier times, had shops selling all kinds of required goods. (courtesy Margaret Lyth)

This card was posted from Uddingston in 1930. The newsagent's shop on the far right is still a newsagents. In 1960 Margaret Lyth struck a blow for feminism by being the first girl employed by that shop to deliver newspapers! At that time the shop was owned by Mr Don McGregor who also supplied books to the public library which was housed, from 1954, in premises near where the hand cart was parked. (courtesy Margaret Lyth)

This view looks north up Old Mill Road and was taken from the junction with Bellshill Road in 1901. It is almost unrecognisable today, the buildings on the right having been demolished to make way for Tunnock's factory. The buildings on the left have been replaced by the church of the Nazarene and car park. Margaret Lyth attended Muiredge Primary School via the Old Mill Road. One of the Tunnock's workers sometimes stood outside the factory and gave passing children misshapen biscuits.

Muiredge primary school derives its name from being at the 'edge of a moor', namely the Muir of Muirmadzean which stretched from Uddingston to beyond what is now the town of Bellshill. When Margaret Lyth was a pupil there during the 1950s Mr Dick was the head teacher. Pupils marched into class to the accompaniment of 'Blaze away' played on the piano by Miss McLaren, or 'Clarabelle' as she was nicknamed. The school celebrated its centenary in 1997.

Above: This picture of Uddingston Cross was taken in the spring of 1961. The van in the far left of the picture belongs to the Scottish Gas Board which had offices and gasworks in Bothwell Road. Behind it is Mrs Burt's sweet shop where children used to spend their pocket money. The premises with the arched doorway were occupied by the Bank of Scotland (now relocated). During the 1950s and '60s the manager was Mr Pettigrew.

Opposite below: The houses in Crofthead Street were built in the late 1890s. The land to the right of the picture was used as the showground. The children nearest the camera are barefoot. Note the very large wicker message baskets. (courtesy Margaret Lyth)

Right: Another view of the 'Candy Man's House', Clydeneuk House, seen earlier. (courtesy Margaret Lyth)

Below: Note the tram and tramlines in this picture of Powburn toll. It was demolished along with Alderside House (between the two telegraph poles on the left) to make way for M74 motorway. (courtesy Margaret Lyth)

This view of Kyle Park was taken from the Clyde Railway Bridge from the Uddingston side of the Clyde, *c*. 1950. Clydeneuk House, demolished in 1963, can be seen in the distance. How rural the area looks. (courtesy Margaret Lyth)

The staff of Uddingston railway station in their Caledonian Railway uniforms, *c*. 1908. The station master is seated in the front row between the two women; seated (left) and standing, (right) are the ticket collectors. (courtesy Margaret Lyth)

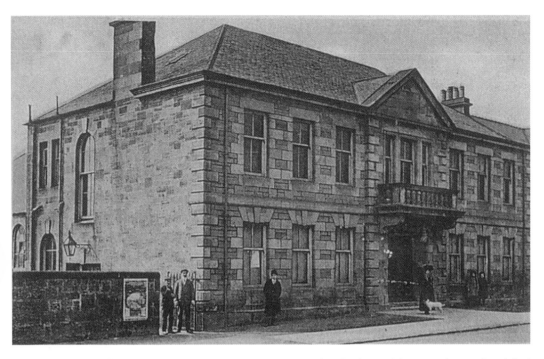

The Public Halls were built in Station Road in 1897 next to the school rector's house. Both were demolished during the early 1960s to make way for the Grammar School extension of 1963. During the 1950s this property was used as a picture house aptly nicknamed 'The Bughouse'. Prior to this use several famous people appeared there including General Booth, who founded the Salvation Army, Ramsey McDonald, Labour's first premier, Harry Lauder and Scott Skinner, the Scots fiddle player. (courtesy Margaret Lyth)

To take this view Mr A. Brown of Lanark had to mount the railway bridge at the top of Sheepburn Road. From 1903 to 1905 there was a massive upsurge in demand for picture postcards so almost any view, as long as it was different, would sell. It is wonderful how old postcards and photos capture for eternity scenes and people in an ever-changing modern world. (courtesy Margaret Lyth)

Main Street — Uddingston

Uddingston Main Street is pictured here during the early twentieth century. Note the condition of the road, the trees and the absence of traffic. The two buildings nearest the camera have now been demolished. The child nearest the telegraph pole is barefoot and the boy carrying a large basket on his head is either selling goods door to door or delivering messages. (courtesy Margaret Lyth)

UDDINGSTON BOWLING GREEN.

Uddingston Bowling Club was founded in 1863 and looks much the same today although the houses in the background have been demolished. This picture is dated 1906. (courtesy Margaret Lyth)

Uddingston's first railway station was opened in 1849 as part of the Clydesdale Junction Railway Co.'s main line south and was taken over by the Caledonian Railway. In the early 1880s the station was still isolated from the village and surrounding farms. In this picture railway staff pose for the photographer while a lady makes a purchase from John Menzies' book stall. This view dates from around 1906; the postcard has the imprint, 'Peter Fraser, Laurelbank.' (courtesy Margaret Lyth)

Gardenside Avenue, looking south, *c.* 1908. The gate has gone. This view was photographed from an upstairs window of number 10 Gardenside Street and the postcard was published by a local newsagent, P. Fraser of Uddingston.

Glasgow Road looks very narrow in this view from around 1910. The boy posing for the camera is armed with a large message basket and may have just completed a grocery order. Before the days of deep freezes and refrigerators groceries were purchased daily, with shops delivering and, for the better off, servants doing the shopping. The advent of two world wars and an increase in car ownership from the 1950s all contributed to change this pattern of behaviour. (courtesy Margaret Lyth)

This postcard of Laurelbank shows that there was diversity of shops when the photograph was taken, c. 1912. Nearest the camera is a confectioner's, followed by William Fraser's tailors and outfitters which has a display of men's flat caps, 'Hooker Doons' or 'Bunnets'; a fruiterer's, stationer's and printer's and a china shop follow. The cart nearest the camera is loaded with bags of coal for delivery by a Cambuslang-based coal merchant. Note how free of litter the street is and note also the wire litter basket attached to the gas lamp. (courtesy Margaret Lyth)

A modern view of Uddingston Main Street for comparison with the earlier scenes above. (courtesy *Hamilton Advertiser*)

Another modern view of Uddingston Main Street with even more cars! Note one name on a shop here that has had a long association with the village: Tunnock's, of course. (courtesy *Hamilton Advertiser*)

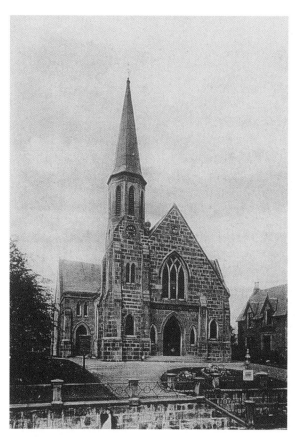

Left: Park United Free church was built in 1863 and is the oldest church in Uddingston. It got its present name in 1900 as it was built on Park feu. Mr John Poynter who owned Clydeneuk House was approached by the gentlemen responsible for the erection of Park church on a park he owned. He granted the feu for the sale of the land, hence Park church. Its first minister was the Revd James Gardiner, from 1879 to 1915. (courtesy Margaret Lyth)

Below: Maxwell Place and Joadja Place on Spindlehowe Road, *c.* 1904. Joadja Place was named after Joadja Creek in Camden Colony, New South Wales in Australia. The word is made up from the first two letters of three Christian names, probably those of the first settlers there, the name being brought to Uddingston by George Watson, the investor who financed the building of Joadja Place on his return from Australia in 1890. This view was taken in winter, as can be seen from the leafless tree. Note also the very muddy road. (courtesy Margaret Lyth)

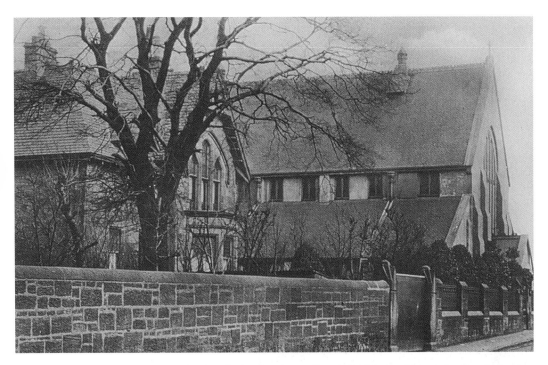

Above: St John's Roman Catholic chapel school was opened in 1883. The Presbytery, chapel and school have now been demolished. A new chapel and presbytery were built in 1980s. Father M. McCarthy who served here was also a president of the Lanarkshire Philatelic Society, of which the owner of this postcard is a member, from 1972-1973. (courtesy Margaret Lyth)

Below: St Andrew's Rectory and St Andrew's Scottish Episcopal church, *c.* 1939. Margaret Lyth and her brother John were born in this house and lived there until their father's retirement in 1975. Their mother, Dorothy Mary Lyth LRAM, gave piano lessons at the house in the room to the right of the front door. Margaret claims she was the worst pupil! The house is now in private ownership. (courtesy Margaret Lyth)

Left: The main door to the parish church was adorned with carved heads of Dr Chalmers, Dr Robertson, Dr Norman McLeod and John Knox. Its formal opening was on Sunday 8 March 1874. (courtesy Margaret Lyth)

Below: Glasgow Road, *c.* 1900. This was part of Telford's road from England to Glasgow. The road has since been widened but is still recognisable from this photograph today. (courtesy Margaret Lyth)

GLASGOW ROAD, UDDINGSTON.

Uddingston Main Street, looking south, *c.* 1905. The Main Street was constructed by Telford through farmland in about 1830. Note the fish and pestle and mortar signs above the shops, reminders of the days when the majority of the population were illiterate. Margaret Lyth can remember these signs and getting shopping for her mother in the fish shop and Flett's the chemist. (courtesy of Margaret Lyth)

This view of Gardenside Avenue has changed little since the 1900s. Gardenside Terrace can be seen at the end of the Avenue and dates from 1895. At one time the land on which the last house in the Avenue resides (left) was used for the tennis court. (courtesy Margaret Lyth)

The house on the left in Brookland Avenue is now part of Redstones Hotel. It was once the home of D.R. Yellowlees Tant and later Sir William Whyte, lawyer who became clerk to Lanarkshire County Council. (courtesy Margaret Lyth)

Spindlehowe Road on an Edwardian summer's day. This card carries the imprint 'D. Morrison, Uddingston' and was printed in Germany. Many postcards of this period were printed in Germany as it was cheaper for the tinting process to be done there. Note the striped pole (middle right) indicating the barber's shop. (courtesy Margaret Lyth)

Posted in Uddingston on the 13 May 1916 this view of Uddingston Main Street dates from around 1910. The buildings nearest camera on the right have now been demolished. Latta's off-sales grocer's shop (left, middle distance) is advertising Bass which, according to popular adverts, was sold in a bottle. (courtesy Margaret Lyth)

This card shows a Glasgow Corporation Tram No. 558 on the Ibrox to Uddingston route prior to 1926 when the Glasgow Road and the Main Street were widened to accommodate trams and their overhead wires. Glasgow 'Caurs' reached Uddingston Cross on the 8 June 1911. The shop to the right of the gas lamp is advertising 'Farriers, Dyers and Cleaners'. (courtesy Margaret Lyth)

Home Sweet Home. (courtesy Margaret Lyth)

This postcard refers to St Andrew's church, as the 'English Church'. This is an error, the church being St Andrew's Episcopal church. The Scottish Episcopal is in full communion with the Church of England and Anglican churches throughout the world. The Scottish Episcopal church has its own college of bishops, the senior of which is the Primus. There is a General Synod and seven Diocesan Synods. This picture was taken by a Valentine photographer in 1936. (courtesy Margaret Lyth)

This view of Bothwell Road is still recognisable today but note the poor condition of the road in this photograph taken in around 1903. Opposite the house on the left is now the Episcopal church, Safeway superstore and Allan's Garage. (courtesy Margaret Lyth)

Bothwell Road, looking south. On the left is one of the entrances to Douglas Gardens. St Andrew's Scottish Episcopal church is situated on the far side of this road, opposite Douglas Gardens. This view has changed little since this postcard was sent to New York in 1908. The gas lamps and 'leerie' have long gone. The leerie was the name given to the man whose job it was to light the gas lamps at night. (courtesy Margaret Lyth)

Uddingston was in the main built in Victorian times and this was when most of the large houses and tenements were erected. Increasing prosperity and improved communications as well as the general amenity of Uddingston encouraged such developments, of which Douglas Gardens was the first to be built in around 1868. (courtesy Margaret Lyth)

The first recorded spelling of the town was Odistoun which appeared on a list of landowners giving an oath of fealty to Edward I of England. Odistoun appears in the 'Ragman's Roll' of 1296, followed by 'Edison' and later by 'Udiston'. The town of Uddingston was built by Walter Oliphant in the first half of the twelfth century to house the servants who worked at Bothwell Castle. This town was made entirely of wood. (courtesy Margaret Lyth)

The Episcopal church was built when the village was expanding. The first priest was the Revd Richard W. Sever who was in charge of an 'Independent Mission in Uddingston'. The mission opened in the Carlelton Hall on Saturday 25 August 1888. Within a year the hall had became too small and after a bazaar held in the McLellan Galleries in Glasgow, which raised £1,000 and donations, the present building was erected with the Revd J.J. McCubbin (Revd Sever's successor) taking the first service on Christmas Eve of 1890.

In 1893 there was an amateur production of *Caste* by J. Robertson in the Victoria Hall in aid of the church organ fund. This event was a success despite boisterous weather and dirty conditions of the roads. The architect was Miles S. Gibson who also designed the St Enoch Hotel in Glasgow. The foundation stone was laid on the 4 August 1890 by Lady Mary Douglas-Home on a site granted by the 12th Earl of Home. Canon Richard Francis Lyth BALTH was rector from 1939-1975. (courtesy Margaret Lyth)

On 15 May 1993 the chancel was damaged by wilful fire-raising. The stained glass window behind the altar melted and had to be replaced. The two manual Blacket and Howden pipe organ was damaged, many of its pipes melting. The organ had been installed in 1895 at a cost of £320. The altar shown above was in the Lady Chapel but the altar which is currently in use was badly damaged and has since been restored. The Cross, the alms dish and some of the altar brasses, but not the altar rail, survived. (courtesy Margaret Lyth)

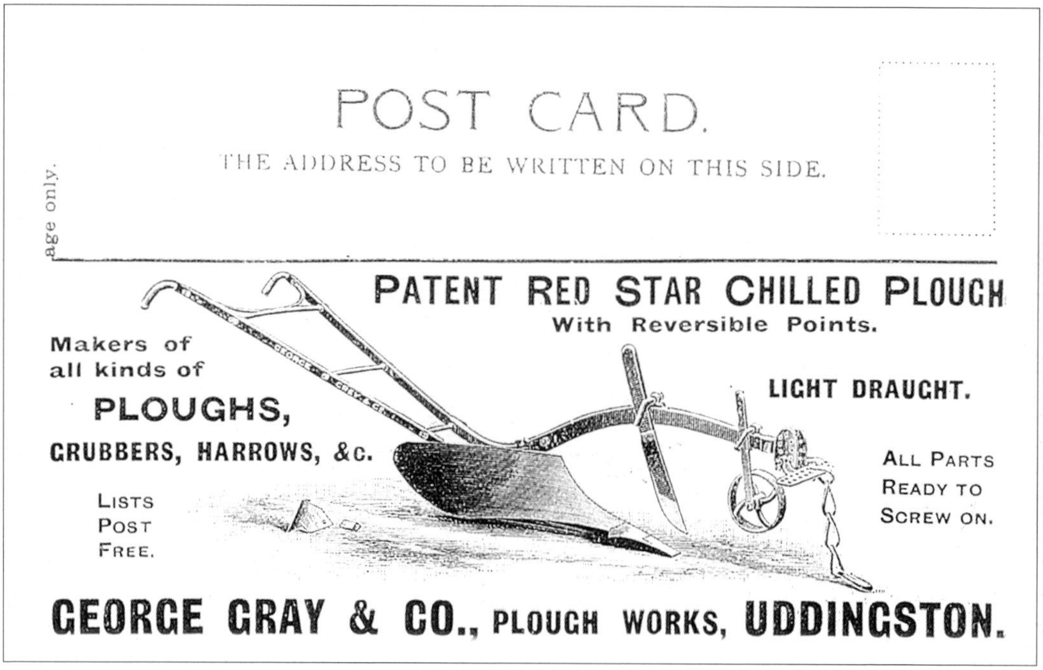

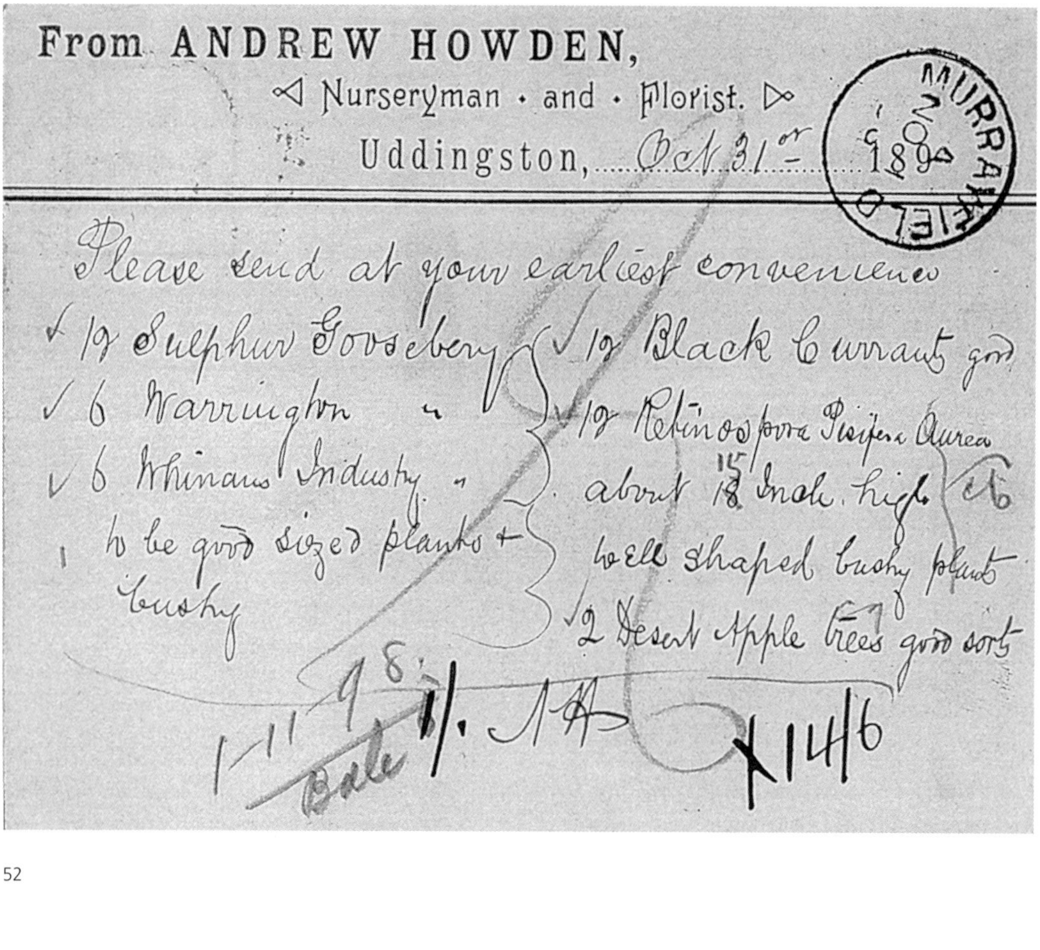

From ANDREW HOWDEN,
◁ Nurseryman · and · Florist. ▷
Uddingston, Oct 31 or 1894

MURRAYFIELD
2 NO

Please send at your earliest convenience

√ 12 Sulphur Gooseberry
√ 6 Warrington „
√ 6 Whinams Industry „
1 to be good sized plants & bushy

√ 12 Black Currants good
12 Retinospora Pisifera Aurea
about 18 inch high √6
well shaped bushy plants
√ 2 Desert Apple trees good sorts

1-11 98
Bale 1/. AH
X 14 6

This postcard is one of the Brown's Series and was posted from Uddingston to Jarrow-on-Tyne in August 1905. The church on the left is Trinity church, now the old parish church. It was built in 1874 on the site of the pond of the Castle Home Farm. The remains of the Home Farm buildings were demolished in 1992. The first minister of the church was the Revd John McKintosh. In the days of the turnpike roads there was a gate across the road just south from where this picture was taken. In the years following the end of the Second World War cows were driven down Bothwell Road and Margaret Lyth can remember them straying into the rectory garden which was not far from where this picture was taken. (courtesy Margaret Lyth)

Opposite above: The front of this postcard shows a view of Loch Lomond in around 1902. On the back someone has pasted an advertisement for George Gray & Co. who from 1850 carried on making Wilkie's Ploughs. John Wilkie (1770-1829) and his son James (1802-1849) gained a reputation for the manufacture of agricultural implements. Their foundry, 'The Big Foundry' was in Crofthead Street, next to the showground. It later became the Victoria Theatre, music hall. (courtesy Margaret Lyth)

Opposite below: In the 1890s Andrew Howden had a nursery at Point Park. This site in front of Cresswell Terrace is now occupied by a children's playground. As well as supplying 'palms suitable for table decorations', he also supplied 'Geraniums, Fuchsias, Carnations, Pinks, Pico tees, Pansies, Violas, Auriculas, Dahlias, Lobelias, Pyrethrums, etc.' The above order from Messrs B. Laird and Sons, Pink Mill Nurseries, Murrayfield, near Edinburgh is for fruit bushes. Howden is insisting on good quality stock. (courtesy Margaret Lyth)

This stretch of Old Mill Road was called School Road and the site of Uddingston's first school was on the left, out of the picture. During the 1950s Mrs Campbell, who lived in Sydney Place, kept hens and sold eggs and some remember them being delicious and often with double yolks. The hens were kept as part of the 1939-45 war effort and continued to be kept during the years of post-war rationing. The building on the left of the picture is Wise's Garage. This view is unrecognisable today. (courtesy Margaret Lyth)

This picture of Loathead Mansions in Main Street was taken by a Valentine's photographer in 1951. The street is a lot less congested with traffic than it is today. Tunnock's shop is still there. Margaret Lyth can remember Archie Tunnock giving her a bun, still warm from the ovens. The remains of these ovens can be seen in the new tearoom today. This postcard was posted from Uddingston to France on the 11 August 1958. (courtesy Margaret Lyth)

Posted from Glasgow in 1941 this card shows a new pavement laid on the right side of the road, having been claimed from the properties on the right side of the street. The building nearest the camera (right) was John M. Williamson's, painters and decorators shop. During the mid-twentieth century Miss Williamson sold hardware and crockery. By the beginning of the twenty-first century the shop had become a restaurant. (courtesy Margaret Lyth)

Bellshill Road, looking west, *c.* 1905. Thomas Tunnock's original shop is next door to that of A. Thomson. 'Pie Tam's' neighbour to the right was A. Donald, who had a 'Meat Mart' there. Both Tunnock's and Donald's are still thriving businesses in the village. (courtesy Margaret Lyth)

Above: This view of Laurel Bank dates from around 1903. Note that this view pre–dates the arrival of the tram service and there is no pavement on the right hand side of the road. (courtesy Margaret Lyth)

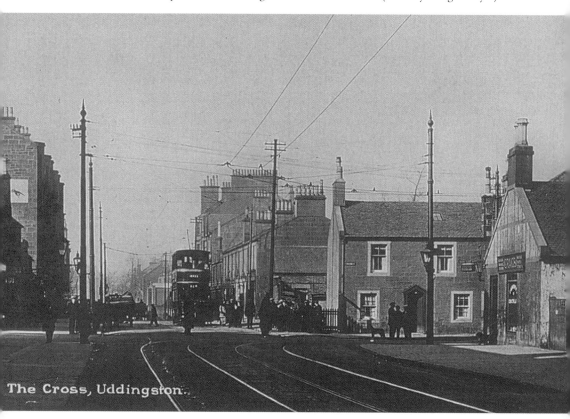

The Cross, Uddingston.

Modern Uddingston Main Street. (courtesy *Hamilton Advertiser*)

Above: The modern Uddingston Job Centre. (courtesy *Hamilton Advertiser*)

Opposite below: A congested Uddingston Cross is pictured here in around 1926. The tram belongs to Glasgow Corporation and is on the Uddingston to Ibrox route. The building nearest the camera is Craig's confectioner's shop which specialised in the sale of 'High class chocolates and bon-bons, home made toffees and tablets'. Opposite (facing the camera) is, 'Simpson's Corner' named after Mrs Simpson, a fruiterer and florist, who owned the property. Craig's is now demolished and Simpson's corner was demolished in 1998 being replaced by flats and shops which include a betting shop and funeral parlour. (courtesy Margaret Lyth)

This thatched summer house was situated in Bothwell Castle Policies. The word 'policies' in Old Scots means 'the pleasure grounds around a mansion', i.e. old and new Bothwell Castle. Sometimes known as the 'Swiss Cottage', it was destroyed by vandals. Although the Policies were designated as a Green Belt by the old Lanarkshire County Council new housing development has been permitted in this area. As a child, Margaret Lyth can remember playing among the foundations of the Swiss Cottage. (courtesy Margaret Lyth)

Due to the rapid growth in population of Uddingston from 750 in 1851 to nearly 2,000 in 1871 it was necessary to build another church in Uddingston as their only church was the parish church of Bothwell, already over subscribed. This concerned the minister, the Revd John Pagan, and after much fund-raising work began under the supervision of R. Halkett the architect. The first tower had to be taken down and rebuilt as it was not built 'according to contract'. (courtesy Margaret Lyth)

This old postcard, converted for use as a Christmas card, shows the Co-operative Stores, and EU church, Uddingston. The Uddingston Co-operative Society was founded as far back as 1861, one of the earliest in Scotland. The first shop, situated in Greenrig Street, is now demolished. This photograph taken in Old Mill Road shows buildings that were completed in 1872. In 1872 the Uddingston Co-operative was paying five shillings in the pound dividend, quite a record. The EU church was erected with local stone and was completed in 1880. (courtesy Ann and Tom Sneden)

This photo shows St John the Baptist's Roman Catholic church in Old Mill Road Uddingston, built in 1902. (courtesy Ann and Tom Sneden)

'The Roman Bridge at Bothwell' was not actually the original bridge here. The is situated near what was once Bothwellhaugh (The Pallis) part of which now lies underneath the loch at Strathclyde Park. The bridge was probably used as a pack-horse bridge crossing the South Calder river. This postcard was posted in Uddingston in 1906. (courtesy Ann and Tom Sneden)

Bothwell Bridge with a tram crossing over it. Much of this scene has changed today. Timothy Pont's map of 1596 shows Clyde Bridge, the name for Bothwell Bridge at this time, built in the early fifteenth century and site of the Battle of Bothwell Bridge in 1679. The main fracas of the battle was fought on the bridge itself, which was much smaller then. The Covenanters were routed by the much superior forces of Claverhouse (Bonnie Dundee) and the Duke of Monmouth. Apparently 500 Covenanters were captured and a staggering 1,200 killed. Many were given support and succour by Duchess Anne of Hamilton at Hamilton Palace. This card was posted in Uddingston in 1908. (courtesy Ann and Tom Sneden)

Above: Bank and Main Street in the early years of the twentieth century. The building in the foreground of the photograph is now the library. In earlier times it was the Bank of Scotland then a dentist's surgery. A hostel was proposed but the idea was well and truly rejected after a heated public meeting. (courtesy Motherwell Heritage Centre)

Right: Park Parish church, Uddingston. (courtesy *Hamilton Advertiser*)

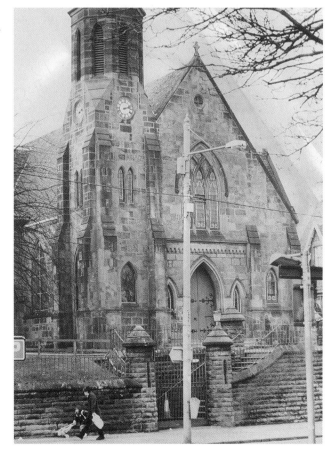

Croftbank House, Uddingston. (courtesy *Hamilton Advertiser*). The name Croft Bank, like Croft Head, comes from the names of cultivated land in the area whose ownership changed with passing of time.

Above: This picturesque thatched cottage stood in Bothwell Castle grounds. When photographed for this postcard in around 1906 it was referred to as the Swiss Cottage. (courtesy Ann and Tom Sneden)

Opposite above: This aerial photo shows Uddingston Cricket Club which was founded in 1883. Note other landmarks in the distance: Strathclyde Park and the tall county buildings seat of South Lanarkshire Council. he new pavilion was erected at the club in 1910 and was formally opened 9 April that year at a total cost of £769 18s 2d by Lord Dunglass. (courtesy Uddingston Cricket Club)

Opposite below: Another view from the air of Uddingston Cricket Club. Can you spot any other landmarks? (courtesy Uddingston Cricket Club)

Uddingston Cricket Club from the air. (courtesy Uddingston Cricket Club)

Opposite above: Map of Uddingston in 1864. Note some familiar names: Porter's Well, Easter Farm, Castlecroft, Crofthead, Croftbank. (courtesy Peter and Susan Murphy)

Opposite below: This old map shows Uddingston in 1898/99. (courtesy Peter and Susan Murphy)

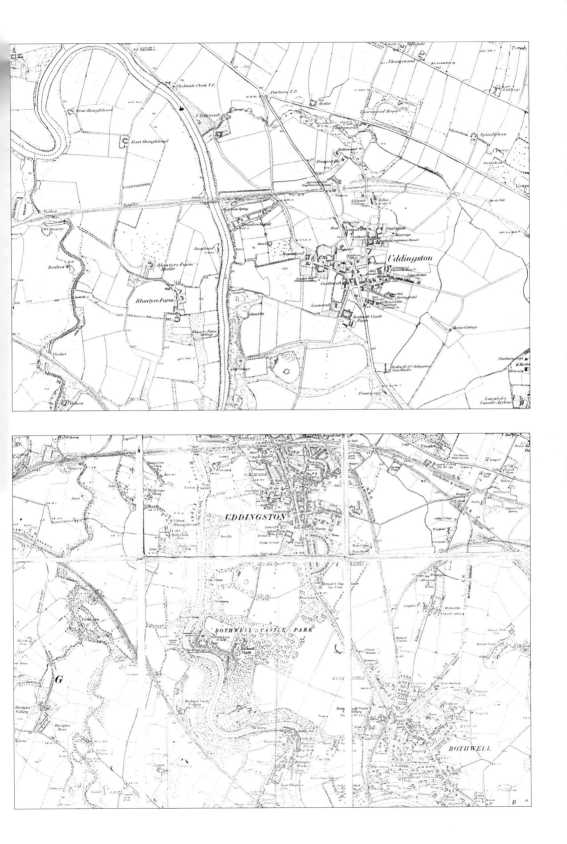

Left: A map of Uddingston in 1912. (courtesy Peter and Susan Murphy)

Below: A street plan of Tannochside and Viewpark, 1982. (courtesy Motherwell Heritage Centre)

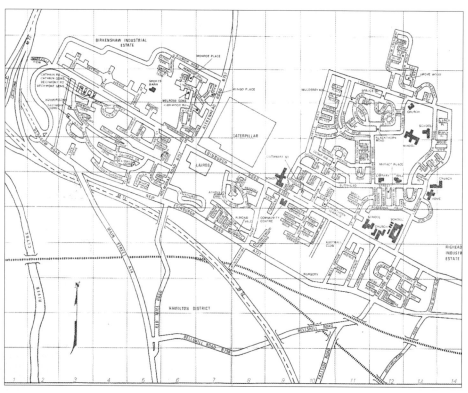

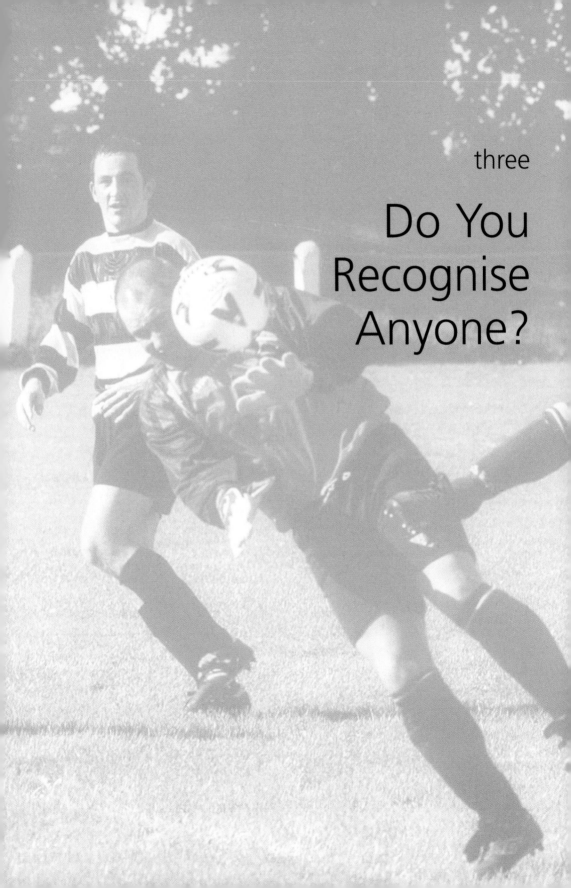

three

Do You Recognise Anyone?

Left: Dorothy Mary Thompson (Mrs Lyth) pictured in 1914. (courtesy Margaret Lyth)

Below: Uddingston second Xl, 1919. The cricket club was founded in 1883 and is still a highly successful club. (courtesy Margaret Lyth)

Opposite above: Birkenshaw 'Police Initiative'. Sgt Scott McEwan, Community Safety Department, is seen with James and Helen Keir from Uddingston, December 2000. (Photographer June Adam, courtesy *The Bellshill Speaker*)

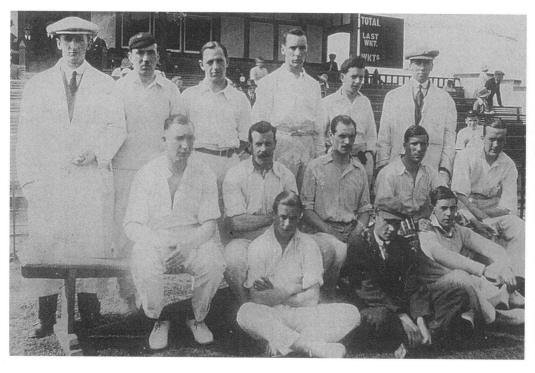

Below: St Columbus Viewpark. Children with Santa Claus, December 2000. (Photographer June Adam, courtesy *The Bellshill Speaker*)

Uddingston coach Mike Hughes with youngsters who went to the Rugby League World Cup, November 2000. (Photographer Nigel McBain, courtesy *The Bellshill Speaker*)

Six young helpers from the Viewpark Ozanam Club receiving the care in the community award for working with children with special needs, June 2000. (courtesy *The Bellshill Speaker*)

It's a knockout! Uddingston Grammar School with Craig Jardine (left), 2nd Uddingston Scouts, battling with Laura Chalmers (right), 2nd Uddingston Guides, June 2000. (Photographer Rodger Price, courtesy *The Bellshill Speaker*)

North Lanarkshire's Deputy Provost Pat Connelly presented the prizes to pupils and teachers from Tannochside Primary School in June 2000. (courtesy *The Bellshill Speaker*)

Above: North Lanarkshire's Deputy Provost, Pat Connelly (centre) presented certificates to students from Viewpark who had recently graduated from the Integra Project, June 2000. (courtesy *The Bellshill Speaker*)

Left: 'The Great Pretenders'. Michael and Gerard McCusker from Uddingston make a few executive decisions at the launch of Enterprise Insight at Glasgow Chamber of Commerce, May 2000. (courtesy *The Bellshill Speaker*)

The lovely ladies of the Uddingston Bowling Club were photographed in May 2000. (Photographer June Adam, courtesy *The Bellshill Speaker*)

The Dedication Bench at Uddingston old parish church, May 2000. Back: Mrs Gelda McCulloch (organist); Andrew McCandlish (church officer). Front: Mrs Anne McKee (McKee Leadership Team for Guild) and Revd Norman McKee. (courtesy *The Bellshill Speaker*)

Above: John Scott (centre) presenting the Supercounty cheque. Around him are: Karen Limond, the Scout Association's Lanarkshire Area Commissioner (rear left), Davie Shaw, Assistant Area Commissioner (rear right) and youngsters from the 2nd Uddingston Scout Group, May 2000. (courtesy *The Bellshill Speaker*)

Opposite below: Birthday Bash, May 2000. Kwik Fit Insurance Services managing director Eric Sanderson and staff celebrate five years operating at Tannochside Business Park, Uddingston. The theme of the party celebrations was Summer Holidays with staff dressed accordingly, in straw hats and sunglasses to sandals and sarongs. The fun day also included free ice cream, a jewellery stall, a cake and candy stall and a birthday travel quiz. (courtesy *The Bellshill Speaker*)

Right: Gregor Clark had a hair-raising experience when he volunteered to have all his hair chopped off for charity. He and his colleagues at Kwick Fit Insurance Services in Uddingston raised more than £500 for a variety of good causes, May 2000. (courtesy *The Bellshill Speaker*)

Below: The Viewpark and Tannochside fund-raising committee of the Cancer Research Campaign presenting the charity with a cheque for £4,200 at St Columba's church, Viewpark, April 2000. Committee president Rose Agnew (back row, third from left) hands the cheque to Julie Hanson who thanked all who supported the committee's efforts. (Photographer June Adam, courtesy *The Bellshill Speaker*)

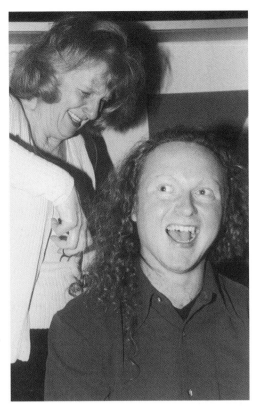

Above: The Mirn Hotel, Fallside, Uddingston, managed by David and Janet Knox for many years. The couple also owned the Moss Inn in Bellshill. Janet (Jenny), now a widow, has recently retired from her later business, Juniors Baby Shop in Larkhall, which she managed with her husband David (Davie) after leaving the Mirn Hotel. Left to right: Jim McDonald, William (waiter) and David Knox. David served in both the Royal Navy and Merchant Navy with distinction in the Second World War, receiving the DSM for his bravery. (courtesy of Janet Knox)

Opposite below: Jenny Knox, now in her eighties, seen here in younger days when manager of the Mirn Hotel in Uddingston. (courtesy Janet Knox)

Right: Another view of Jenny Knox in the Mirn Hotel, conversing with a customer. (courtesy Janet Knox)

Below: Fallside Action Group, Local Heroes Care Awards, March 2001. Left to right: Fallside Cllr Charles Hebenton, Action Group Chairman Donald Murn, John McKenzie, Margaret McKinlay, Anne Main, Provost Barry McCulloch, Jenny Mollen, John Stark (resource worker with North Lanarkshire Council Community Services Department), Elizabeth Robertson and Cirsteen Williams. (courtesy *The Bellshill Speaker*)

Tom and Ann Sneden on their wedding day 6 June 1958. Ann was brought up in Uddingston (née McKirdy) and the couple live in Motherwell. (courtesy Ann and Tom Sneden)

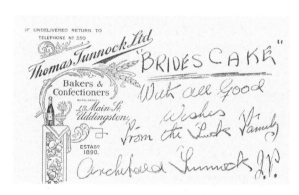

Above and left: The wedding cake, a present from the Tunnock family to Ann McKirdy of Uddingston on her marriage to Mr T.E. Sneden. (courtesy Ann and Tom Sneden)

Right: Uddingston daffodil competition winner Chloe Brown, aged seven years, from Muiredge Primary School with Provost Alan Dick, February 2001. (courtesy *The Bellshill Speaker*)

Below: Bowling at Uddingston Bowling Club, April 2001. (Photographer Nigel McBain, courtesy *The Bellshill Speaker*)

Happy Harriers, these young runners from St John the Baptist Primary School, Uddingston have every reason to smile after their performance in the Hamilton District Schools Cross Country Championships at Bent Park, Hamilton. The girls trained very well to win both the Primary 6 and 7 team contests. Overall, St John the Baptist was the second team behind Hamilton College. (courtesy *The Bellshill Speaker*)

Gala line up. Smiles from Uddingston Civic Week Queen Julie Fleming and her court as they prepared for the 2001 year event which took place from June 9-17. Julie was a pupil at St John the Baptist Primary School and was crowned at Uddingston Grammar School on Saturday 9 June. From left to right: Shona McDonald, Muiredge Primary (lady-in-waiting); Graeme Watt, St John the Baptist (escort); Ross Turpie, Muiredge Primary (boys' champion); Julie Fleming, St John the Baptist (queen); Emma Boyle, Muiredge Primary (lady-in-waiting); Kieran Smith, John the Baptist (Escort). (courtesy *The Bellshill Speaker*)

An Uddingston firm awarded for superior standards. Paterson's of Greenoakhill on Hamilton Road supplies many of McCarthy and Stone's retirement developments with precast blocks. Left to right: Steve Wiseman (Regional MD, McCarthy and Stone) and Alan Perry of Paterson's. (courtesy *The Bellshill Speaker*)

The Golden Wedding of Mr and Mrs Curran, Viewpark. Well done! (Photographer June Adam, courtesy *The Bellshill Speaker*)

Above: Thorniewood United, August 2001. Note the familiar Uddingston name on their strip. (Photographer Nigel McBain, courtesy *The Bellshill Speaker*)

Left: The Headliners! Local group, the Big Elastic Band, preparing to top the bill at the Glasgow West End Festival in June 2001. The band is lead by local man Harry Barry and includes his daughters Kate and Jane. The photographer was Nigel McBain, whose father Charles is an excellent photographer and who has himself worked for many years in this field. (courtesy *The Bellshill Speaker*)

Opposite above: Thorniewood United Football Club versus Ashfield Football Club, October 2001. (Photographer Nigel McBain, courtesy of *The Bellshill Speaker*)

A Thorniewood striker challenges the Ashfield keeper, October 2001. (Photographer Nigel McBain, courtesy *The Bellshill Speaker*)

North Lanarkshire Council workers Alan Smith and Danny Cox (foreman) at Viewpark Gardens. (courtesy of *The Bellshill Speaker*)

Party time! A dinner, dance and cabaret at St John's Baptist church Parochial Hall, organised by 474 Council (Viewpark) of the Knights of St Columba for local people with special needs, Uddingston, November 2001. (courtesy of *The Bellshill Speaker*)

'We shall remember them'. People of the Parish of Bothwell, Uddingston, remember the fallen of two great wars on the 11 of November 2001. (courtesy *The Bellshill Speaker*)

The Job Centre in Uddingston. This photo depicts the more modern, personal approach to helping folk back into the workforce or those changing career direction. Uddingston and surrounding areas, as elsewhere in the country, have seen the rise and demise of sources of employment. (courtesy *Hamilton Advertiser*)

These smiling
youngsters had taken
part in an indoor
athletics competition
held in the leisure
centre in Larkhall. Ten
teams were involved
from other schools
in the area with St
John the Baptist's
pupils winning bronze
medals. Uddingston,
March 2002. (courtesy
The Bellshill Speaker)

Pupils at St John the Baptist school taking part in a cookery project, March 2002. What happy, smiling faces! (courtesy *The Bellshill Speaker*)

Tunnock's honoured eight members of staff who had each achieved twenty-five years of service in the bakery at a reception held at Scottish Television headquarters in Glasgow in March 2002. Managing director Boyd Tunnock and actor and celebrity angler Paul Young presented them with watches and certificates. Mr Tunnock paid tribute to the workers' loyalty and the high standards they had maintained over the years. Front row, left to right: Kathleen Carlin, Lillian Wilkie, Lena McQueen. Back row: Paul Young, Bob Cook, Muriel Higgins, Boyd Tunnock, Jennifer O'Brien, Bobby Lynch, Steven Kidd. (courtesy *The Bellshill Speaker*)

Members of the Fallside Play Scheme Committee show off their certificates after completing a committee skills course, which were presented by Kirsteen Thompson (far right), co-ordinator at the Community and Voluntary Organisations Council who facilitated the course. (courtesy *The Bellshill Speaker*)

Muiredge Primary School photographed after making it through the auditions for the Supercounty
Primary School Choir Festival, June 2002. (courtesy *The Bellshill Speaker*)

Uddingston Cricket
Club on a very wet
day in July 2002.
Treasurer Neil Lockhart
(third from left) with
Uddingston and
Glasgow West End
Cricketers, who seven
competition was washed
out. Uddingston Cricket
Club every summer
invites anyone who
wants to play cricket
for fun days. The people
who come are made
up into teams of seven.
(Photographer Nigel
Bain, courtesy *The
Bellshill Speaker*)

Some of the people who turned up to see the launch of the recycled garden area at Viewpark Nursery, August 2002. All material shown had been on its way to a landfill site including bricks, stones, a kettle, etc. (courtesy *The Bellshill Speaker*)

Diamond Wedding couple David and Lilly Brown of 21 Simpson Court, Uddingston received a commemorative scroll and flowers on behalf of South Lanarkshire Council from Provost Alan Dick and Cllr Patrick Morgan, August 2002. (courtesy *The Bellshill Speaker*)

Above: Local young people with Cllrs Jim McCabe and Charles Hebenton at the official opening of the Fallside Youth Shelter, September 2002. (courtesy *The Bellshill Speaker*)

Left: Members of the Uddingston Pride Group, Walter Silcock, Jean Wardrobe, Mary Scott and Pat Donnelly, beside the village Christmas tree in December 2002. (Photographer Nigel Bain, courtesy *The Bellshill Speaker*)

Opposite above: Back together! Former captains Mae Kerr and Helen Scott cut a cake to mark the seventy-fifth birthday of lst Tannochside Girl Guides. Members past and present attended the reunion at Viewpark parish church hall to celebrate the occasion. (courtesy *The Bellshill Speaker*)

Taken in December 2002. Christmas came early for Anne Higgins of Viewpark when council leader Cllr Jim McCabe presented her with a £10 Christmas gift from North Lanarkshire Council. Looking on are (left to right) 'Santa's little helpers', Jade Dunlop, Kelly Ann Grady and Tacy McGlinchie from the First Stop Shop in Viewpark. Anne was among 60,000 senior citizens in North Lanarkshire to receive a gift from the council. For the seventh year running, the £10 gift was paid to senior citizens during the last week in November and the second week in December. The gift was payable to both men and women aged over sixty. (courtesy *The Bellshill Speaker*)

Above: This photograph of the Lyth family was taken in the 1950s. Cannon Richard Thomas Lyth, BALTH, was the minister of St Andrew's Scottish Episcopal church in Uddingston from 1939 to 1975. His wife, Dorothy Mary Lyth, taught piano. Also pictured are Margaret and John Lyth.

Left: 'Pie Tam' outside his shop. An illustration from a Tunnock's cake box. (courtesy Margaret Lyth)

THOMAS TUNNOCK LTD.
34 OLD MILL ROAD · UDDINGSTON
GLASGOW G71 7HH · SCOTLAND

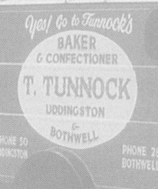

four
Tunnock's

Tom's shop it stands in Bellshill Road
He sends you his best wishes
He'll give you a treat
That Kings could eat
In clean and bonny dishes

Fair are the flowers of Summer
Fair are the upper skies
But dearer to the epicure
Are Tom's Mutton Pies

Should you wish a Wedding Cake
Or wish for something Special
Tom is the man you always can
Rely on for a Social

Should e're you donner through our Toon
and pangs o' hunger seize you
Tunnock's Shop will surely cope
With all it needs to please you

Above, left and right: These verses were printed on Tunnock's bags when Tom Tunnock started the business in 1890. (courtesy Margaret Lyth)

Above: This painting, entitled *Tall Ships on the Clyde* by B. Dobbie, was reproduced as a postcard in 2002 (with an added detail in the right hand corner) to celebrate the fiftieth anniversary of Tunnock's Caramel Wafers. The original painting is owned by Boyd Tunnock MBE and reflects his own interest in sailing. The painting was on loan to the Burnside Gallery, Brodick, and the Isle of Arran in 2002. (courtesy Margaret Lyth)

Opposite above: This old postcard, dated 1910, shows 'The Cross', Lorne Place, Uddingston. In this shop the Tunnock legend began. The founder of the firm was Thomas Tunnock, who was born in Uddingston in 1865. The name Tunnock goes back for several generations within the Parish of Bothwell. In 1890 Thomas purchased these premises on the Bellshill Road from his savings for £80 and began trading under his own name by December of that year. (courtesy Boyd Tunnock)

This old photograph shows (left to right) Alice, Mary and Tom Tunnock in the back shop at Main Street, Uddingston in 1916. Thomas married Mary Mitchell, aged twenty-one, in 1892. The couple took up residence in Fairview Place in Uddingston. Their son, Archibald, was born in 1895 and daughter, Alice, in 1903. Archibald (Archie) later carried on the business. By 1906 Tom employed six boys, including his own son. (courtesy Boyd Tunnock)

This view shows the ovens inside the bakery at Loanhead Mansions, in the Main Street, *c.* 1920. The premises in Lorne Place had been destroyed by fire in 1912 but the resilient Thomas built the new bakery at Loanhead Mansions. Sadly Thomas died in 1920 at the early age of fifty-four. Pictured in this photograph are David Spiers (left) and Archie Tunnock. At the time of Thomas's death Archie, like so many other young men of his generation, was away serving his country in the army. On his return home after being demobbed he learned the tragic news of his father's death from a friend who met him at Central Station in Glasgow. His father had died two weeks prior to his return. (courtesy Boyd Tunnock)

Tunnock's staff Whist Drive Dance at Uddingston Masonic Hall, 11 April 1933. The Tunnock family through the years have been well thought of not just for their business acumen but also the considerate and fair way they have treated their staff. (courtesy Boyd Tunnock)

Right: Staff at the bakery making pastry shells for mutton pies, May 1934. Remember them, with the hot juice running down your chin? Yum, yum! (courtesy Boyd Tunnock)

Below: Archie Tunnock, like his father before him, was also extremely successful as a purveyor at local functions bringing his own very personal touch to events. The 'Steak Pie' was always one of the favourites but he would also supply other pies, pickles, sausages, tea and arrangements for the tables. The years between the wars were great decades for the family business, Archie himself on some occasions working eighteen hours a day. Note the pristine uniforms of the staff in this photograph taken in May 1942. Archie married Margaret Boyd, a local farmer's daughter, in 1926 and their first son, Thomas, was born in 1929. A second son, Boyd, followed in 1933 and today he is the head of the family. (courtesy Boyd Tunnock)

Mr Archie Tunnock and staff in May 1924. (courtesy Boyd Tunnock)

The Tunnock family and staff in May 1948. (courtesy Boyd Tunnock)

In the 1940s Archie Tunnock arranged four gymkhanas. The most memorable one was held in 1945. Its purpose was to raise funds to welcome home from the services the brave men and women of Uddingston at the end of a horrendous war. The grand sum of £2,500 was raised, enough to give each returning man and woman a gift of £5. Archie's natural flair and his marvellous way of promoting and advertising events resulted in people flocking in from miles around. Archie was renowned for being a generous man. (courtesy Boyd Tunnock)

Another scene from one of the gymkhanas held in the 1940s. (courtesy of Mr Boyd Tunnock)

Women working in the Tunnock's factory in the 1950s. Tunnock's cakes and biscuits are world renowned. (courtesy Boyd Tunnock)

Staff working in the bakery in 1956. In this view are Rena ? (left), May Logan (second from left), Meg Crawford (front right), Cathie Quinn (rear, facing camera) and John Brannan (rear right). (courtesy Boyd Tunnock)

Tunnock's staff pouring out hot caramel in the early 1950s. Left to right: Agnes Roy, Annie McSeveny, Barbara Love. (courtesy Boyd Tunnock)

In this photograph from the late 1950s Archie Tunnock is seen handing out Christmas presents to the staff. He was a larger-than-life character regarded affectionately by the hundreds who worked for him. He was a JP and served as a Lanarkshire County Councillor. (courtesy Boyd Tunnock)

Above: This photograph, taken in 1955, shows Archie Tunnock (centre) celebrating his sixtieth birthday with his staff. His son Tom is sitting in the front row, to his right. Archie had a special tricycle with a light on the front, useful because he would still be working when the 'backshift' clocked off at night. Quoting once, 'I've a tricycle that takes me quickly round, because everybody wants to talk to me and I want to get past them to see how the mallows are doing'! He knew all his staff on first name terms, always calling the female workers 'girls' no matter what age they were. Archie died at his home on 17 July 1981 aged eighty-six years. (courtesy Boyd Tunnock)

Tunnock's New Daylight Bakery in Old Mill Road. The extension on the far left of the photograph was built in 1969. (courtesy Boyd Tunnock)

Right: A new extension going up at Tunnock's New Daylight Factory in 1965. (courtesy Boyd Tunnock)

Opposite below: A view inside the bakery in 1960. In 1947 Tunnock's held a grand opening of their New Daylight Bakery which was built nearby in Old Mill Road. Further extensions were to follow in 1962 and 1965. Interestingly, the factory now occupies the site of the old bakery where Thomas Tunnock served his apprenticeship back in the 1880s. In 1924 Archie opened a new, larger tea room in the Main Street, taking over dwelling houses above the shop. The shop is still there today. When working in Uddingston in the 1960s at nearby Cockburn's Chemist (next to Gow's shop) my treat on a Saturday was having my lunch in the tea room upstairs. (courtesy Boyd Tunnock)

Archie Tunnock checking the mail in his office. Note the portrait of his father Thomas behind him. Archie held a keen interest in cricket and through the years his benevolence towards the Uddingston club was enormous. Archie's two sons carried on the tradition of supporting the club. Another love of Archie's was his cars which included three Rolls Royce's and a Rover. At his large mansion he had a small zoo with corgies, sheep, lambs and many exotic birds. Archie and his wife Margaret Boyd were regular attenders of the old parish church. Archie donated two beautiful stained-glass windows to the church in honour of his father Thomas. Mr Boyd Tunnock, Archie's younger son, still attends the family church and has held the position of church elder. (courtesy Boyd Tunnock)

Left: One of Tunnock's bright red delivery vehicles at old Bothwell Castle. Archie had a marvellous flair for advertising and publicity. (courtesy Boyd Tunnock)

Opposite above: Another of Tunnock's vehicles at Bothwell Castle. One of the firm's specialities was wedding cakes. Archie saw most of the brides-to-be when they called with 'mother', such was his personal interest and attention to detail. (courtesy Boyd Tunnock)

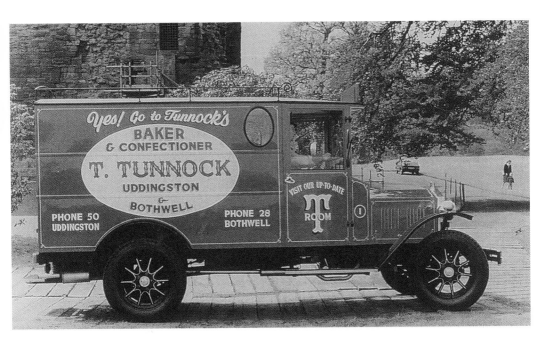

Two generations of Tunnocks. Left to right: Tom Tunnock, Archie Tunnock (father) and Boyd Tunnock. Thomas was born on the 19 June 1929. Archie and Margaret's eldest son was encouraged from an early age to take an interest in the firm. In 1955 he married Margaret Gilmour and the couple had two daughters, Carol and Patricia. Boyd, the younger son, was born on the 25 January 1933. In 1957 Boyd married Anne McLay. They have three daughters, Lesley, Karen and Fiona. (courtesy Boyd Tunnock)

One of the Tunnock's delivery vehicles outside the Daylight Bakery in Old Mill Road. (courtesy Boyd Tunnock)

A view inside the Daylight Bakery in Old Mill Road in 1983. (courtesy Boyd Tunnock)

Another view from inside the Daylight Bakery in Old Mill Road in 1983. (courtesy Boyd Tunnock)

A view of the Daylight Bakery in Old Mill Road in 1964. (courtesy Boyd Tunnock)

Above: Staff working in the bakery in the 1960s. Do you recognise anyone? (courtesy Boyd Tunnock)

Right: Archie Tunnock and Alice McPherson with a display of Tunnock's goodies at a trade exhibition in the 1950s. (courtesy Boyd Tunnock)

Opposite above: Bakery staff packing Tunnock's Coconut Snowballs in the 1960s. (courtesy Boyd Tunnock)

Opposite below: Staff photographed outside the bakery in the 1950s. (photographer Charles McBain, courtesy Boyd Tunnock)

In 1990 the staff presented a cake to the family as they celebrated 100 years of business achievement. (courtesy Boyd Tunnock)

This is the front of the programme for Uddingston Grammar School's Annual Athletic Sports held at Meadowbank Park in 1932. Note 'Teas, Ices, Confections' were supplied by A. Tunnock. (courtesy Boyd Tunnock)

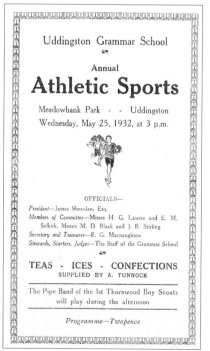

Uddingston Grammar School

Annual

Athletic Sports

Meadowbank Park - - Uddingston

Wednesday, May 25, 1932, at 3 p.m.

OFFICIALS—

President—James Sheridan, Esq.
Members of Committee—Misses H. G. Lawrie and E. M. Selkirk, Messrs M. D. Black and J. B. Stirling
Secretary and Treasurer—E. G. Macnaughton
Stewards, Starters, Judges—The Staff of the Grammar School

TEAS - ICES - CONFECTIONS
SUPPLIED BY A. TUNNOCK

The Pipe Band of the 1st Thornwood Boy Scouts will play during the afternoon

Programme—Twopence

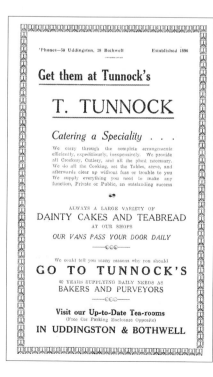

'Phones—50 Uddingston, 28 Bothwell   Established 1890

Get them at Tunnock's

T. TUNNOCK

Catering a Speciality . . .

We carry through the complete arrangements efficiently, expeditiously, inexpensively. We provide all Crockery, Cutlery, and all the plant necessary. We do all the Cooking, set the Tables, serve, and afterwards clear up without fuss or trouble to you We supply everything you need to make any function, Private or Public, an outstanding success

ALWAYS A LARGE VARIETY OF

DAINTY CAKES AND TEABREAD
AT OUR SHOPS

OUR VANS PASS YOUR DOOR DAILY

We could tell you many reasons why you should

GO TO TUNNOCK'S
40 YEARS SUPPLYING DAILY NEEDS AS
BAKERS AND PURVEYORS

Visit our Up-to-Date Tea-rooms
(Free Car Parking Enclosure Opposite)

IN UDDINGSTON & BOTHWELL

Above: Tunnock's products go all around the world. This photograph, taken in the 1980s, shows Mr Boyd Tunnock holding a box of Caramel Wafers during a visit from some agents for overseas sales. Boyd was awarded the MBE in 1987. (courtesy Boyd Tunnock)

Right: This photograph was taken in 1987 aboard HMS *Fearless* and shows Boyd Tunnock and some of the ship's crew promoting Caramel Wafers. Boyd has a great love of sailing and finds it a relaxing occupation after long hours in the factory. His yacht is called *Lemarac* which is 'Caramel' written backwards. Boyd is a member of the Clyde Cruising Club and has served on its committee, part of the time as Flag Officer. (courtesy Boyd Tunnock)

Success is not new at Tunnock's Bakeries, Uddingston

THIS MONTH WE HAVE SHIPPING SPACE BOOKED FOR
120 TONS—6,730 LARGE CASES OF
TUNNOCK'S CHOCOLATE BISCUITS
OUR AUGUST EXPORT SHIPMENTS ARE AS FOLLOWS:—

DESTINATION	NUMBER OF CASES	PORT	VESSEL
ST. JOHNS, NEWFOUNDLAND	300 Logs.Choc. Bis. 50 C.W Choc. Bis. 100 C.W (4 pack) Choc.Bis.	Closing at Liverpool 14th August	Per 'NOVA SCOTIA'
NEW JERSEY	1200 (6 x 48) C.W Choc. Bis.	Closing Glasgow End August	Per 'AMERICAN LANCER'
GUYANA	125 C.W.B. Choc. Bis.	Closing at London 12th August	Per 'NATURALIST'
PENANG	150 C.W. Choc. Bis.	Closing at Grangemouth 18th August	Per 'BENMHOR'
KUWAIT	200 C.W.B. Choc. Bis. 200 Logs. Choc. Bis.	Closing at Glasgow 15th August	Per 'BALTISTAN'
HONG KONG	600 C.W. Choc. Bis.	Closing Grangemouth 29th August	Per 'BENARMIN'
NEW BRUNSWICK	150 Log. Choc. Bis.	Closing at Manchester 6th August	Per 'MANCHESTER EXPORTER'
TRINIDAD	140 C.W.B. Choc. Bis. 40 C.W. Choc. Bis.	Closing at Glasgow 18th August	Per 'PLAINSMAN'
PENANG	240 C.W. Choc. Bis.	Closing at Grangemouth 18th August	Per 'BENMHOR'
HONG KONG	500 C.W. Choc. Bis.	Closing at Grangemouth 29th August	Per 'BENARMIN'
VANCOUVER	50 Piper Choc. Bis. 50 C.W. Choc. Bis. 25 Piper p/p Choc. Bis. 25 C.W. p/p Choc. Bis.	Closing at Glasgow 12th August	Per 'DINTELDYK'
KUALA LUMPUR	400 C.W. Choc. Bis.	Closing at Grangemouth 29th August	Per 'BENARMIN'
KUWAIT	900 C.W. Choc. Bis.	Closing at Glasgow mid August Loading date later	
JAPAN	500 Part-coated C.W. Choc. Bis. 500 Part-coated C.W.B. Choc. Bis.	Closing at Glasgow 18th August	Per 'JASON'
W. GERMANY	9 C.W.B. Choc. Bis. 6 Logs Choc. Bis.	To be delivered to London—August	Loading date later
BENGHAZI	20 C.W. Choc. Bis. 50 Log Choc. Bis.	Closing Liverpool end August	Loading date later
SINGAPORE		Closing Glasgow/Grangemouth end August	Loading date later

P.S.—WORK IS PROGRESSING RAPIDLY ON OUR LATEST THREE-STOREY EXTENSION TO OUR BAKERY WHICH, WHEN COMPLETED IN THE AUTUMN, WILL HELP TO MEET THE EVER INCREASING DEMAND FOR OUR PRODUCTS IN BOTH THE HOME AND OVERSEAS MARKETS.—470 EMPLOYEES HAVE ALSO TO FILL 32 OF OUR VANS WITH FIFTY VARIETIES OF CAKES AND BISCUITS DAILY.

This advertisement for Tunnock's in *The British Baker* magazine, August 29 1969, shows the extent of the company's overseas trade at the time. (courtesy Boyd Tunnock)

TUNNOCK'S
CHOCOLATE CARAMEL WAFERS

17 TONS OF QUALITY CHOCOLATE USED EVERY WEEK.
6½ TONS OF GOLDEN CARAMEL AND THOUSANDS OF DOZENS OF CARAMEL WAFERS MADE DAILY.

4 Layers Golden Caramel
5 Layers Crisp Wafers

Some people THINK we only make

TUNNOCK'S
CHOCOLATE CARAMEL WAFERS

BELOW IS A LIST OF CAKES, NOT COUNTING THE COUNTLESS VARIETIES OF SCONES AND TEABREAD WE MAKE DAILY IN OUR UP-TO-DATE BAKERY AND FACTORY AT UDDINGTON EMPLOYING 538 PERSONS

TUNNOCK'S NEW DAYLIGHT BAKERIES, UDDINGSTON
Phone UDD 3551 (4 lines)

P.S.—We do not insert our advertisements in a boastful manner, but to assure our customers old and new we want their orders.—A.T.

An advertisement for Tunnock's in the *Glasgow Illustrated*, March 1964, takes space to show the large range of cakes and biscuits made by the firm at the time. (courtesy Boyd Tunnock)

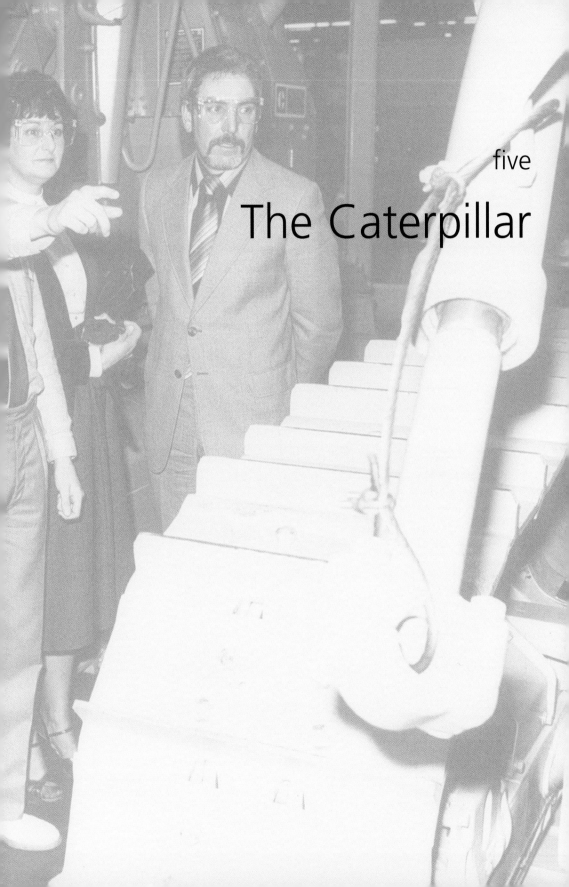

five

The Caterpillar

The Caterpillar Plant at Tannochside. Caterpillar, a world renowned company, came to the area in the 1960s. The plant at Tannochside had a huge workforce and was by far the biggest employer in the area. Sadly the plant is no longer there and, like the closure of Ravenscraig in Motherwell, caused huge unemployment in the area. The Caterpillar was a forward-thinking American-owned company with modern ideas that enhanced the working conditions for its workforce. The plant closed in late 1987. (courtesy Motherwell Heritage Centre)

A group of Caterpillar workers that went on an outing to Helensburgh with the Bowling Club in the 1960s. Among them is Ivy Littledyke Robson (third from right) and her husband Norman Robson (back row, fourth from left). Norman Robson was a member of the management staff at the Caterpillar plant. (courtesy Norman Robson).

A group photograph for the Caterpillar management at the Tannochside plant in the late 1950s. Norman Robson is third from right on the front row. (courtesy Norman Robson)

The maintenance department at the Caterpillar plant in the 1960s. This department won top safety awards for three years running out of all the company's plants worldwide. Norman Robson is in the second row, and was a section manager at the Caterpillar plant. (courtesy of Norman Robson)

A presentation event at the Caterpillar plant for a leaving member of the Quality Control Department in the 1960s. Unfortunately we don't have a record of who she is.

This photograph taken in the 1960s shows the Caterpillar Fire Team from the Tannochside plant. The team won countless awards in local competitions. (courtesy Norman Robson)

The wedding of William and Elizabeth Mair in 1965. William ('Wullie'), who came from Leith, worked at the Caterpillar plant at Tannochside and was active in the union. Sadly William died in 1968 when his son (William) was only six months old and his colleagues at the plant were kind and supportive to his young widow at the time. His son (my nephew) went on to do extremely well in the academic field and graduated from Glasgow University. William now lives in Broxburn with his wife Helen and their two children, Duncan and Fiona. (courtesy Elizabeth Third)

A photograph was taken in 1979 as new apprentices were beginning their training in the Caterpillar plant at Tannochside. Parents were escorted around the plant by invitation of the company and here Stephen Porteous (a new apprentice) explains some of the processes to Norah, his mother, and Ronnie, his father. Stephen finished his apprenticeship and when the plant finally closed went on to work in New Zealand and then Australia, making a good life for himself. Both Ronnie and Norah were stalwart members of the Motherwell Historical Society; sadly, Ronnie has recently passed away. (courtesy Norah and Ronnie Porteous)

The Caterpillar Cricket Team from the Tannochside plant in the 1960s. Norman Robson, who took a huge interest and personal involvement in all of these plant sports, is fourth from left in the back row. Born in Doncaster in 1924, Norman worked initially as an electrical engineer in the mining industry, a job he continued to do during the Second World War. He later came to Tannochside to join the Caterpillar company in management. (courtesy Norman Robson)

Right: The Caterpillar Fire Team at the Tannochside plant. (courtesy Norman Robson)

Below: Men from the Caterpillar Bowling Club attending a tournament in the 1960s. Norman is second from left. (courtesy of Norman Robson)

Above and below: These two photographs, taken in the 1960s at the Caterpillar plant, show an open day for the wives and families of employees. The photograph above was taken in the medical department. There was an emphasis on good health at the plant and this department was well equipped and employees were encouraged to follow a healthy lifestyle. The photograph below was taken in the IBM room. (courtesy Norman Robson)

These photographs were taken during the Caterpillar occupation in 1987. The machinery shown here was used for making tractor parts. The decision to close this very productive and successful plant down seemed incredible, but sadly it did happen in spite of the determination and courage of the men who fought the closure. The news broke on the 14 January 1987 to a shocked and angry workforce. The shop stewards immediately announced their intention to occupy the plant, forming a Joint Occupation Committee. The support for the occupation in and around the area was overwhelming, with rallies, protest marches and a soup kitchen. The last meeting to discuss the occupation of the factory was held on the 27 of April 1987 when it was decided to end the occupation of 103 days: the image below was taken on the last day of the occupation. Work resumed on the 27 April 1987 and continued until the plant's closure later that year. The agreement the men reached was no compulsory redundancies until the 16 October 1987 and an early retirement plan for those over fifty. The blow to the area was the loss of 600 jobs. (courtesy of Motherwell Heritage Group)

six

Easter Farm

Easter Farm is reputed to be one of the oldest buildings in Uddingston. The house is now the home of Peter and Susan Murphy who have restored the house and worked hard to retain its historic character. They have also been active in researching the history of the house, its outbuildings and the immediate area around it. The house was built by Andrew Jack, a clever entrepreneur who, with the passing of time, amassed great wealth and owned a great deal of land in Uddingston which is still referred to as Jack's Land (Laird Jack) and known in the 1700s as the Lands of Birkenshaw. The present house is probably the result of at least one rebuild, perhaps from, or over, an original single-storey building as the ceilings in the upper floors are higher than those downstairs. The front and back of the house may have been reversed at some time in its history because the date plate is now at the back of the house. (courtesy Peter and Susan Murphy)

Off to the ball! This photograph was taken outside Easter Farm where friends gathered before heading off to Edinburgh for a Millennium Ball. The military ball reunited some First Gulf War veterans and other personnel from both the Regular Army and Territorial volunteers. Susan Murphy (middle) had eleven years of service with Queen Alexandra's Royal Army Nursing Corps and reached the rank of major. 205 Scottish Field Hospital (RAMCV) Corps is manned mostly by the Territorial Army in conjunction with the Royal Army Medical Corps. Her husband Peter is second from left. (courtesy Peter and Susan Murphy)

Peter Murphy, of Easter Farm, was born in Townhead, Glasgow in 1933. He is an astute business man whose enterprises have taken him to far-flung places in the world where, no doubt, his Glasgow wit and humour have endeared him to many. Peter and Susan have now established a time line for the previous occupants of Easter Farm from Andrew Jack's building and naming of Birkenshaw House in 1782. The brother-in-law of Andrew Jack, James Patterson (trust factor) also seems to have played an important role in the history of the house. Andrew Ford rented it from the late 1800s and it was he that changed the name to Easter Farm. An original Easter Farm was once on Old Mill Road. The Patterson trust sold the house to the Mullholland family in 1947 who remained owners until 1998 when Peter and Susan bought it. (courtesy Peter and Susan Murphy)

The grandchildren of Peter and Susan Murphy on an Easter egg hunt at Easter Farm in 2002. They are, from left to right, Liam, Kaigleigh, and Ryan. (courtesy Peter and Susan Murphy)

Left: Susan Murphy walking the dogs outside Easter Farm. The byre at the back offered accommodation as the chimney, still in position, is cut from a solid piece of Bothwell Pink sandstone, which pre-dates 1700. The house is full of original features and some of the farm implements used there are now on show at Hamilton Museum. The cottages are older than the farm and date from around 1600. The inn which stood nearby was a rest halt for passing coaches on the Carlisle to Glasgow coach road. It is said that twelve coaches arrived and left on a daily basis. (courtesy Peter and Susan Murphy)

Below: A view of the kitchen at Easter Farm, with Susan cooking. (courtesy Peter and Susan Murphy)

A picturesque scene at the entrance to Easter Farm, looking towards Knowhead Cottages, in the 1950s. The man leading the horse is a member of the Mullholland family who purchased the property from the Patterson Trust in Adelaide, Australia. The builder of the house Andrew Jack married into the Patterson family. A notable inn once stood on the opposite side of Porterswell. After entering Porterswell, on the right, a number of buildings once stood; one belonged to Merchant Eglinton, who had a ten-loom weaving shop and sold cloth and groceries. Andrew Jack owned a shop too on the left-hand side which acted as an unofficial post office (the post office being in Bothwell). (courtesy Peter and Susan Murphy)

This photo taken in the 1950s shows Easter Farm as a working farm, at milking time. (courtesy Peter and Susa Murphy)

The old fireplace in the present kitchen at Easter Farm today. A story attached to the earlier house on this site is that in 1746 Charles Edward Stuart (Bonnie Prince Charlie) was reputed to have stopped on the disastrous retreat from Derby. A row of single-storey cottages would have been typical of this area at the time, built with rough rubble, roofed with branches from the trees and then thatched. A group of six like this stood off Old Glasgow Road, near Gardenside and were known as Johnnie Rae's Throat. (courtesy Peter and Susan Murphy)

Above: Easter Farm in the 1960s, looking west towards Easter Mews, originally part of the farm. (courtesy Peter and Susan Murphy)

Right: Andrew Jack, the son of Andrew Jack, senior, who built Birkenshaw House in 1782. Andrew Jack was the First President of the Co-operative Movement in Uddingston (1861-1881). His father built Birkenshaw House in 1782 on land where previously stood a single-storey house. Andrew Jack, who built Birkenshaw House, died on the 15 December 1847 and is buried in the graveyard at Bothwell church. After his demise his brother-in-law became factor to the Jack estate and proceeded to rent the house and farm out to a family by the name of Ford. The Ford family were dairymen and farmed the land, renaming it Easter Farm. The Jack family have a lineage in the area going back to medieval Scotland and were farmers beholding to the Bothwell estate. In old records they are noted as vassals and on one occasion got into trouble for failing to supply Glasgow Cathedral with wax for the tomb of St Mungo (or St Kentigern) and his mother St Thenaw or St Enoch. The culprits were threatened with excommunication. (courtesy Peter and Susan Murphy)

Mr ANDREW JACK.
First President—12th December 1861 to 15th December 1881.

127

Other local titles published by Tempus

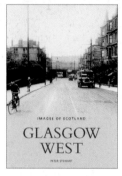

Central Glasgow
PETER STEWART

The look and life of Central Glasgow, once the Empire's Second City, are vividly captured in this collection of photographs which spans a hundred years or more. Hard times and happier days are reflected in over 200 images, many of which have never been published. With sections on the Clyde and the vanished shops, hotels and tea rooms of the central part of the city, this is an essential, and beautiful, guide to the city in times past.

0 7524 0675 2

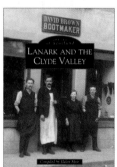

Glasgow West
PETER STEWART

This collection of more than 200 images, part of Peter Stewart's best-selling series on the city, explores the history of the west of Glasgow over the last 150 years. Much has changed over that time, but many of the area's sweeping Victorian and Edwardian terraces retained their grandeur as fashions, faces and vehicles evolved around them. This nostalgic volume will delight anyone who has lived or worked in the area and provides a valuable social record of the way things were in this thriving city.

0 7524 3658 9

Lanark and the Clyde Valley
HELEN MOIR

The site of an early Scottish parliament, Lanark and Clyde Valley was also where William Wallace began his battle for Scottish independence against the English. Over the two centuries portrayed in these beautiful photographs, New Lanark became world famous as it evolved from a typical mill town into a radical model workplace, the Scottish International Aviation Meeting of 1910 introduced 'flying machines' for the first time to Scotland and Milton Lockhart Castle was transported, stone by stone, to Japan. This book will delight all who know and love the area.

0 7524 1757 6

Larkhall
HELEN MOIR

This collection of more than 200 archive photographs and old advertisements takes the reader on a fascinating tour of Larkhall as it once was. From Millheugh to London Street, Harry Dawson to the infamous Hamilton dynasty, and with particular focus on the loom weaving and mining industries, it gives a flavour of Larkhall's community as it was many years ago.

0 7524 1530 1

If you are interested in purchasing other books published by Tempus, or in case you have difficulty finding any Tempus books in your local bookshop, you can also place orders directly through our website

www.tempus-publishing.com